Text Copyright © 2013 by Montrell D Goss
Illustrations Copyright © 2013 by Joshua Dudley
All rights reserved. No part of this book may be used or reproduced in any manner whatsoever without written permission except in the case of brief quotations embodied in critical articles and reviews. Printed in the United States of America.

From My Pain To My Passion
By Montrell "God's Instrument" Goss

Cover Page By: Joshua "Big Snubb" Dudley

Graphics By: Jay "Raz" Roberts

Success: Acknowledging self-worth in your everyday life by reaching your full potential to accomplish all goals. Not being defeated, but rather defeating the world against all odds. Success cannot be bought, but can be worth a lot. I am a witness that dreams do come true; so live your dream and be successful. Don't let yesterday stop you from being a better person today.

God's Instrument

Bio

"My heart overflows with a beautiful thought! I will recite a lovely poem to the king, for my tongue is like the pen of a skillful poet." (PSALM 45:1 NLT)

Montrell grew up in a single parent household with three older brothers and a younger sister. Him being the youngest, growing up without a dad really affected him. Living in the cold streets of Portland, a city with not much to do, Montrell tried to occupy his time by playing sports and spending time with his family. As an adolescent, Montrell spent most of his time in bible club and church. As the years went by Montrell, started to get stronger in faith and began to believe that God was telling him he should write. By the age of nineteen Montrell got serious about his writing.

You see everybody has a story to tell, but some people just don't know how to tell it. Montrell was one of those people. Until one day God spoke to him and said, "It's easier to get your feelings out if you write them down on paper." After that, he began to write a book. By the

age of twenty, he released his first book called "Judgment Day." In 2011, he released his second book "I'm Not a Writer I Am Poetry." Montrell's goal is to win souls, make disciples, and help people release feelings that they hold within. He believes that people shouldn't let yesterday stop them from being better people today. All in all, Montrell wants to show that, through everything you go through in life, there will always be a better day.

Tale of Contents

21. Dedication

23. My Angel

25. Thank You

27. A Cry For Help

29. Let Down

31. Feeling Blue

35. Isolated

37. Hiding In The Shadows

39. In My Zone

43. The Hurt

45. Jesus Or Self Pleasures?

47. Friends? Or Nightmares?

51. Boxed In

53. Picture This

55. Battle

57. Keep Going

59. You and I

61. You Got To Go

65. What You Know About?

67. God Heard My Cry

69. Always There

71. Addicted

75. Share Your Story

79. The Answer

81. Picture This Part 2

83. Can I Cry?

85. Pray Before My Day

87. Home Sweet Home

89. Amen

91. P.O.L

93. Look Alike

95. My God

97. From The Womb

99. From The Womb To The Road

103. My Time My Future

105. Overcoming Obstacles

107. Blue Print

109. From My Pain To My Passion

111. Your Dream My Calling

115. My Life My Passion

117. I'm Ready Lord!

119. Off To The Races

123. Lost and Found

125. Controversy

129. Stop Lying

131. Broken

135. Was It Really Love?

137. Isn't She Lovely?

141. A Perfect Gentleman

145. Help Wanted

149. Alter Call

151. The Prayer

153. Bonus Page

155. Letter to My Dad

157. Letter To My Father

159. You Can't- Woman

161. You Can't- Man

163. No More

167. Moments of My Deepest Regrets

171. I Salute

173. Layover

177. Introduction To: Why Me?

179. Why Me? (Joy)

183. Why Me? (Fear)

185. Restored

189. Write Your Own

191. Write Your Own

193. Write Your Own

195. Write Your Own

Dedication

I want to dedicate this book to my grandma Lizzie B Varner; my grandma taught me so much about life. She was a hard worker, she was caring, and she always finished what she started. My grandma showed me the true value of a dollar. She showed me that money can last as long as you want it to. If you just did the things you needed, and not the things you wanted. My grandma's not here with me to give her a signed copy of this book or to watch me on stage, but I know she is with me in spirit, and she is watching over me. I'm glad God blessed me with such a wonderful grandma. Love and miss you, I will always be grandma's baby boy.

My Angel

Time is lost by different problems and different pains, but it's not always a bad thing because when you go through things sometimes you gain. In this case, it was different because we lost something, but my grandma gained a lot, and now she does not have any problems and her pain will stop. We might feel a little pain, but that will soon be over and, I felt like before grandma past she was trying to say that she wanted the family to be closer to each other. So let's become the family she wanted us to be, and grandma is still with us so everything we do she will see. Let today be the day we stop all the fussing and fighting because she was not about that, she was all about family. Grandma was a simple woman that cared for everyone, and she was the best. She is in a better place now where there's peace and lots of fun, and God already had angels watching me, but now I have another one. So grandma take care of the family and make sure we're alright, and be our guardian angel while we rest our heads at night. Forever missed

Thank You

God I want to tell you thank you for everything you did for me. You died and then rose again, just to set my soul free. Without you in my life, I don't know where I would be, maybe in jail or maybe just running the streets. My dad wasn't there, but you took care of me, and I just want to tell you thank you for helping my mom live a life stress-free. I want to tell you thank you for always being there, even when I didn't believe in you, you still were there. Thank you for blessing me with many different gifts and talents. I'm going to keep praying and reading my bible so I will have that spiritual balance. God you brought me a long way, and there's no way I can repay you, but I'm going to try my hardest to be a godly man. The last thing I want to tell you is, I love you and thanks once again.

A Cry For Help!

Let me start off by saying forgive them father because they know not what they do. In my life, I've been confused by love and pain so much that at times, my mind can't even distinguished the two. I never knew that those that love you so much could behind your back inflict so much pain on you. As I go through these rough times, I ask my Lord and savior to help me and fill me up, so I can find my break through. Even though they have inflicted pain on me that's not something that I want to do, but instead I want to help them make it through. They say when you're going through things you usually take it out on the person that's the closest to you. So you laugh, you scream, any way you can hide your true feelings. What God has shown me is, to not bottle them up, and even though it's hard at times you have to just reveal them, face them and don't let pride get in the way when your mind is telling you to ask for help so you can overcome them. So as you see I started off by talking about myself but quickly switched and took the focused off me. Because I was one of those people that use to hide my feelings and this poem, is a cry out. To ask is there anybody out there that can help me.

Let Down

God I feel I let you down and all my smiles turned into frowns. You were the only one there for me when no one else was around. It's like I turned my back on you I turned away from your grace, and every time you would send a sign to try to help me I would just throw it back in your face. God I really do want to change, but I can't do it without you, and you told me that all I had to do was trust and never doubt you. God I know you're by my side and by my side you will always be. And I just want to say thank you because you helped me to become me.

Feeling Blue

Down and out

Feeling blue

Mind racing what shall I do?

Living life

Feeling wrong

Lonely beat to a lonely song

Use to smile now I frown

The world on my shoulders

Has turned upside down

Long day's sleepless nights

Battling dreams enjoying nightmares

Wait! I'm fighting the wrong fight

Living in sin just feels so right

Long road home, but I will be alright

Caught in the world but I should be different?

But this is all I know

So I have to search what's missing

Down and out

Feeling blue

Got an answer from you know who

Jesus Christ, savior of my life, showed me right, he showed me wrong

Now I'm fine living life

Different beat to a different song

And I can't wait to get to heaven because there's no place like home.

Isolated

All alone, by myself, isolated, where's everyone else? Stranded, helpless, where's my road side assistant? Broken need fixing. But how can you fix a heart when all the love is missing? Thoughts and dreams, nightmares and reality. Happy, sad, smiles, angry. Laughing, crying, bi polar, now this can't be me. I need Faith, trust, belief, salvation. Please Jesus forgive me and help me with the things that I'm facing. I want to feel your love, your grace, forgiveness upon me lord. I'm willing to let you order and control me. Fill me; lead me on the path that is right, with wide arms. I'm coming, just please hold me tight. Bad thoughts are gone and love has come, living for God but still under construction.

Hiding In The Shadows

Dark, gloomy, quiet and frightened.
Alone, shaking, balled up, wondering, is this the end.
I've been hiding in shadows so long I forgot what lights look like.
I have been in the dark so long I forgot what days look like.
I was always told to let my light shine so everyone can see. Matthew 5: 13-14 was one of the first scriptures that was read to me. Still I was hiding in the shadows, waiting for my next move, knowing I should have been letting my light shine daily because God already paid my light bill way before I was even consumed. Assistant, persistent and instead of giving up I need to be more consisted. On letting Gods light shine through me, and I shouldn't care or worry about how the schools, work place, or even my community views me. So no more hiding in the shadows, it's time to stand out and let my light shine. I need to go against all odds and make my way to the front line. No matter what it takes I will make my way. Because God has been shining through me and I need to let my light shine every day.

In My Zone

I'm trying to get back in my zone, clear mind refreshed and focused. I tend to find myself falling back losing focused, then snap out of it and tell myself you have to control this.

Control my life that is, because my life had been ruined by drugs, pornography, even fornication.

I'm just being modest because these are only a few things that I'm facing.

I lost faith and belief in the Lord

Even started believing money was my God

Thought I was doing well because I had money in my pocket, thought I was on the center stage spot light on me, but it was an empty room and I was like dang that's odd.

I felt like I got everything in the world that will make me happy

Drugs, sex, and money until the lonely feeling, comes back, and I realize that those things don't make me.

Matter fact I realize those things are doing nothing but harming, hurting also breaking me. After realizing this, it helped me get back in my zone, to my passion, and that's

writing poetry, now that God has control of me, I'm ready to be the man God has called me to be. God's Instrument

The Hurt

The Hurt, the sadness, the rage, and loneliness. The anger, the headaches, the tears, and the heartbreaks. Frustration, confusion my life feels like an illusion. Like "this can't be really happening it has to be a dream," "maybe if I go to sleep when I wake up I won't see the same things." But now I'm in a nightmare, I'm scared, I'm frightened. The horror, the vision, is taking me back to that night when I lost sight of God I couldn't see him nor hear him, I thought I was close, but my faith showed me I was nowhere near him. The selfishness, the greed, the doubt, and unbelief. Has haunted me every night as I lay and try to sleep. The fear of going to hell has never really crossed my mind until that day doctor told me my life was almost over and I was running out of time. So I prayed, I believed, I had faith, I went to church. But I soon realized I'm only doing this because I'm hurt. It's fake, it's unreal, a fairy tale, and its fiction. And I'm burning inside because every day I feel the conviction. Now I'm lost with no compass, nor direction. And all I had to do with stay close to the one that save me back when. I was feeling the hurt, the sadness, the rage and loneliness. Yes, Jesus, the King of kings, Alpha and Omega, The Almighty, yes pure holiness. Hopefully God will give me another chance because I don't want my life to end like this.

Jesus Or Self Pleasure?

We're going through life, feeding into our sinful desires. Asking God for all the wrong things because that's what we think our heart's desire. But does our hearts desire pain? Because every time we sin, it's like Jesus being hung again. But we don't care because our self pleasure makes us happy and makes us feel good. We fall in love with that short term pleasure instead of falling in love with the things we know we should. Like praying, reading the bible, and trying to get closer to God. Naw, that stuff don't matter unless we going through something or feeling a little pain because that's the only time you hear the name Jesus, other than us using the Lord's name in vain. Now isn't that a shame! And we famous for saying, "if we could go back we wouldn't do the same things." But how about we look at our lives and learn from them, instead of doing the same things. So how about you? Look at your life and see if there's anything you can do to make your life better. And while you're thinking about those things, ask yourself this one question: what do you love more, Jesus or self-pleasures?

Friends? Or Nightmares?

I was always told to follow my dreams, but I'm like how when my life is filled with a bunch of nightmares, a bunch people saying they got your back but deep down inside they're the ones stabbing you in your back cause in reality they don't really care. A bunch of people trying to trip you to make you fall and when you do they try to kick while you're down. Made a promise that they will always be there but when you're at your low points of life, they're nowhere to be found. A bunch of clowns is what I call them. Same people that down talk you for your situations but will never try to fix their own insecurities or their own problems. But if something bad was to happen to you they get the crying and once again, they swearing, they will always be by your side. In your mind your like Mmm hmm, yeah ok, why would I believe you now when last time all you did was lie? But let's put that aside. You were there to hand me that liquor and handed me that gun when it was time to ride. To sell those drugs with me, and yeah when all those girls wanted to the party you were right there with me. Now that I think about it that's not the people I want around. I want people that's going to hold me accountable for my actions and keep me away from things that's tearing me down. Friends that pick me up when I fall and encourage me to fight harder and to stand firm on the next go around. As I pray and ask God

to place those people in my life. I thank him for the friends I have now and thank him for taking those nightmares out my life.

Boxed In

Lost, only to find that I'm blinded by the true way of living because the way that I'm living does not show the example of Christian living. Though I have asked for forgiveness also repented to be forgiven, I still have to die to myself daily in order to be different.

Trapped, only to realize that my mind set is not pure yet, and I have to pray for a reset or in other words to be renewed because I'm so tired of going in circles and I knew a new mind, not a mind that's being reused.

Caged, only to figure that there's no escape from the world itself but I will soon break these chains that I have been wearing for years because I was scared to face God, my struggles and my fears.

Boxed, only to determine that I'm out of shape but now I'm working out, going to church, reading my bible I had to change everything around. Because I kept asking myself why would I want to live boxed in? In a world that's round.

Picture This

Picture Jesus getting a scar for every time you sinned, and you didn't ask for forgiveness or even drop to repent to Him. Do you think you would be able to see Jesus' skin? Or would you just see all the marks that you have placed on him? Picture you were there that day Jesus died on the cross, and you saw Him get hit with sticks and stones just so your sins would be lost. And you telling me that you can't praise the one that paid the ultimate cost? Now picture you saw Jesus bleeding and you never saw so much blood. Would you give Him your shirt? Or would you leave His body covered in blood? Now I know it's a lot to think about, but let's think about what God did for us, He gave his only son just to show his love for us. Now picture if he never did that, our lives would still be filled with sin. So I'm thankful that he did that because when I mess up, I can ask and Jesus will forgive me of my sins. When you picture something it might take a while, so you have to use your brain. You see it took me a minute, but when I saw the picture my whole life changed. So ask God to show you the picture because it really helped me, but I can't tell you everything I saw. I have to just let you see.

Battle

Battling this sickness mind going crazy, praying asking God help me, these pains are tearing me apart daily. Situations got me down but yet starting to amaze me. Questioning like I been sick since a pup, why couldn't they have figured this out when I was a baby? I refuse to throw in the towel, I grab it, use it to wipe off my sweat. Keep fighting, look up thank God for my situation and ask what shall I do next? Because I won't give up, I won't let this beat me, and with God on my side nothing can and will defeat me. Praying for God's love, his grace to bring me peace. This sickness, these pains I rebuke with hopes that they be released. Viewed as a distraction trying to get me off my path, holding on to faith is the best thing I've learned in the past. I use to feel the wrath then I got convicted. Was introduced to God and I've been following him ever since then. Since the day, I was born I had a rare conditions, but I soon realize God has the upper hand, so I prayed I watched, I waited, and I listened. Now I'm 27, and I'm still battling this sickness mind still going crazy, but God got my back started off as a kid now I'm God's child, and he takes care of me daily.

Keep Going

When you feel like giving up that's when you get your second wind and go on, you see I was that kid in that dark tunnel that didn't see the light but felt like it will come soon so I told myself to go on. Growing up I couldn't spell, handwriting was horrible, and I could barely read, read Philippines 4:13 I can do all things through Christ who strengthen me. So I knew one day those things I would soon achieve. Hard nights brought along puddles of tears not being able to succeed, but I kept the fight going not even understanding why, but I knew God had a plan for me. So I prayed and prayed for God to help me, felt like I heard his voice say "my son I'm here for you just keep your faith and stay near me." So that's what I did kept the faith and kept trying, knowing in my head God's will, will be done at the right time because he has perfect timing. Days went on I started notice things changing I was writing better, and I was also reading more books. Start crying, fell to my knees and thank God for prayer because prayer, hard work and dedication is what it took. I soon got my calling I was to become a writer I would write poetry. And I never gave up even when, "you will never be a good reader or writer" was told to me.

You and I

I woke up to my future, you woke up telling dreams.
You talk about what you want or never had, I talk about what I have or have seen.
You think money is success I say that's a lie.
I say success is accomplishing things you never thought you could achieve, and money is just here to help you survive.
You say money over everything I say God over the universe.
You have to say vulgar words when you do poetry or rap, I can write a master piece, and I don't have to curse.
You trying to fit in with the world I'm trying to start new trends.
Your trying to find you identity, I'm trying to improve being a godly man.
You give up when things gets hard, I pray and try again.
You live life scared to show you true feelings; I release my hurt through my pen.
You use to be me, till I decided to switch my mind set; now I am working to better my life, and I haven't looked back yet.

You Got To Go

For years I have allowed you to be in my life, you broke my spirit, made me cry, you even made me turn on things and people I love.

For years, you manipulated me to do things even though I know they were wrong. Oh go have sex, smoke and drink. You know you want to tag along.

For years, you have gotten me further and further away from finding myself, finding my identity. Told me you knew what was best, you told me you were a friend of me.

For years, I listened because I was scared to take a stand and make a change, but those days are over and I will stand and let you know I'm tired, and I will change.

For years, I have been this person because I was scared to be different, but sometimes it's ok to be, and I figured out that, that's what I was missing.

It's been years since I kicked Satan out my life and chose to walk with Christ, the one who died for my sins and the one who never left me even though I wasn't living right.

Even though it's been years the enemy stills tries to sneak in and try to get me to think about the times that we

spent, but I pray and shake that off because even though I thought those things felt good, there's no better feeling than the love God sent…Jesus Christ

What You Know About?

What you know about Genesis to Revelations?

What you know about Adam and Eve?

What you know about Jonah and the whale?

What you know about parting the seas?

What you know about David and Goliath?

What you know about turning water to wine?

What you know about healing the sick?

What you know about making a man see that was once blind?

What you know about walking on water?

What you know about the Ten Commandments?

What you know about the five loaves and two fish?

What you know about dying then rising?

I know I asked a lot of questions about what you know, and you might know about everything I asked, but the question is not what do you know but what does God know about you?

God Heard My Cry

As I patiently waited, God heard my cry. He's there when I need him; my handkerchief to wipe my eyes. As I pray to him daily, he gives me a firm place to stand. And I lean not on my understanding, but I put my faith and trust in him. As I live this life, it seems like it gets harder every day, but I P.U.S.H. Pray until something happens because I feel that's the only way. I can get over struggles. The way I can release my pain and fear, and every time I began to stray away the Lord still remains near. To whisper in my ear and remind me that I wouldn't have made it this far if it wasn't for him. So I can't give up. I can't turn my back now. I have to stay strong in this fight and get back up if I fall down. 'Cause Jesus didn't stay down he was hung. He died and he got back up 'cause there was a plan for his life, and it didn't include giving up. So don't throw in the towel now. Cry out to the Lord he hears it. And even if you don't see a change now, God's working; just believe it.

Always There

You were always there, and that means a lot, at first nobody believed in you, but you still rose to the top. I couldn't get nothing pass you, you was on me tough, my life was a disaster till you said "enough is enough". You kept me close to your side never letting go. You know everything about me things that people will never know. When I was ready to give up you, sat me down, talked to me and said keep going. That hill was tough to climb, but I kept going, had to keep on pushing even though fatigue was showing. You change my life in so many ways, and I thank you for it and haven't figured out by now, I'm talking about my lord just to let you know it. No matter what you're going through God will always be there, just call on his name, don't worry about your background God doesn't even care. He will help you through just pray and wait. And my advice is to do it now what's the point to wait.

Addicted

At age 5, I was introduced to drugs. Saw something in my parent's hands that was glass like, grew up and realized it was a glass pipe. So you can say I was addicted to drugs my whole life, right?

At age 7, I was touched by my uncle. But growing up all I heard was, family is all you have in this life, I was like my family did that to me, so something just isn't right. So you can say I was addicted to sex my whole life, right?

At age 9, I became obese. My mom work 3 jobs, so she wasn't at the house, she just use to leave money on the counter for us to buy pizza or take out. So you can say I was addicted to food my whole life, right?

At age 11, I got my first x-box. Played all the games with the shooting and running from the cops. Grew up and the game became reality, and I felt like I couldn't be stopped. So you can say I was addicted to violence my whole life, right?

At age 13, I was introduced to Adam. Heard the story about him eating the fruit, God called it sin because it was something he forbid him to do. So you can say sin will always be in our lives, right?

Through all our sins and addictions, God died on the cross so we can have a second chance. So I guess you can say I will forever be addicted to true love for the rest of my life, right?

Share Your Story

Nobody knew because of the smile that I've been hurt, and it's been haunting me for years.
It hurts to think about it, hurts more when I try to share. Wondering one day will I ever release this pain in there? So, I hide behind my laughter, my smiles even material things, hoping nobody will see the hurt and I will never have to share those things. Things that broke me down and forced me to change, things that made cry, made me bleed, and at times I thought I was over it I looked deep inside and the anger still remains. The fight to get better was the worse, I couldn't win. Felt like, when I started to get better my hurt always came out to show it had the upper hand. I always thought to myself, I would rather struggle through life than to let my situations cause me not to live at all. But every time I tried to fight through I would just get hit hard by life and fall. I should of let it out a long time ago I should of just told my story, but I let my anger get the best of me one day and now I'm not alive to tell my story. I died in a fight who would have known lucky punch. That anger had me grounded and instead of walking away my anger reassured me that I ain't no punk. I should have just listened when my friend Gods Instrument told me to share my story because you never how your testimony can relate to someone else's story. The moral of this is I was that kid that didn't want to tell my

story, and that was just a visual reality check I didn't die, but that was the road for me. I want you to know after I finally shared my story, I became a better man and now I feel God's glory.

The Answer

It's called a struggle it's called pain, it's called falling down and getting back up with no tears or no shame. It's called trying harder even when you feel you've tried your hardest. It's called taking a chance because you never really know you can't finish something if you never took the time to start it. It's called being a great follower in order to once lead. It's called being a great leader so you too can teach someone to lead. It's called believing in yourself even when it's easier said than done. It's called being prepared to answer the call and show up when your time comes. What I have learned through all this is, my struggle has lead me to my success and my pain is temporary so it won't last long. I have fallen down plenty of times, but I get back up because God gives me the strength to move on. I took a chance with my faith and became a great follower. My leader is a great leader, and he's also my father. I believed in myself when nobody else did, and I'm blessed to have written 3 books, something I can't say, not to many people I know have done. My clock is still ticking so I can't stop now and I want to leave you with this, even with all I go through the love Jesus have for me is the reason I keep going and the reason I smile.

Picture This Part 2

Yeah I know in part one I said I was going to let you see, but I have to let you know the things God has just revealed to me. The cross, the hands, the feet, the head. The sweat, the tears, the blood that was bled. The names, the spit, the hurt, and the pain. All this to save us, but we still live the same. The parties, the fights, the sex, and the drugs. Doing these things just searching for love. We ask He forgives, and we do it again. It's like we just want to keep living in sin. Why? I don't know, but there has to be a reason, and I will figure it out! 'Cause now is my time, it is my season. I was put here to make a difference so I will complete my task. To help me do that, I have used my own experiences. Right now, my future, and also my past. My past tells a lot about where I came from and how I'm different today. The present shows how I'm living and how I'm trying to do it God's way. The future, well, I don't have much to say but that I'm going to heaven and through the son is the only way. So everything I said in the beginning wasn't just something for me to write. Jesus dying on the cross brought me out the darkness, and now I see the light. Now I hope you saw the picture and asked God to change your ways. And even if your change doesn't come over night, keep praying because your change will come one day.

Can I Cry?

Eyes watering, looking real glossy, almost to my breaking point and nothing and no one can stop me. I just need to let it out been holding back these tear, past hurt, past pain I been holding on these feelings for years. Where's my shoulder to cry on? Who do I talk to for comfort? Don't trust people, so I hold it in, man, I'm so tired of this God please help me I don't want to be hurt. As one tear drops my heart cries more, please God send someone to me help me please let this broken heart be restored. I wish I could just bandage it up like a scratch when I fall, but it's much more difficult than that. Feels like I need a new everything, heart, legs, brain and all. God I might not ever understand the true meaning this, but I just want to ask you one question. Can you just bend down for a sec? I just need a shoulder to cry on for a little bit. Can I cry?

Pray Before My Day

Woke up this morning and I didn't take time to pray. Showered, washed my face, brushed my teeth and went on about my day. Day was kind of rough. Problem after problem, situation after situation were coming with no directions on how to solve them.

I lost my cell phone, locked my keys in the car everything was just going all bad. I was hungry but couldn't eat because I reached in my pocket and I realized I lost the few dollars that I had. My job was trying to fire me, school called because my kids were acting up. I'm really about to lose my mind literally if this day don't start picking up. Finally got home made dinner and tried to rest, but my mind was everywhere, so I started thinking about times I was blessed. Went to sleep and woke up the next morning energized. Showered brushed my teeth and got them sleep boogers from my eyes. But before I left the house this time I took time to pray because tomorrow is never promised, at least I can do is pray and thank God before I start my day.

Home Sweet Home

Home sweet home, what nice words to my ears? A place where I can be comfortable sit back relax and be myself without fear. It's a place where I can feel welcome every time I walk in because they don't judge me because of the way I dress or because of the color of me skin. A place where I can take my family, and also invite my friends. A place that I will always call home until the very end. The church, my church, also known as my second home.

Amen

I pray for the lost, the sick, and the shut in.

I pray for the families that have no food and have been left with nothing.

I pray for those that's hurting and fighting different pains.

I pray that God shows mercy and their loved ones be changed.

I pray for the stressed, depressed and lonely people.

I pray that the challenged and disabled that they all get treated as equals.

I pray for the tears and for all those with sorrow.

I pray for today because we're never promised tomorrow.

Amen

P.O.L

Praise on the street corner
Praise in the church
Praise where the lost is the sick, the healed, the hurt
Praise when the blessings come
Praise when things are bad
Praise for all the feelings you have the happy ones and the sad
Praise when you're in the storm
Praise when you get out
Praise because you kept your faith and not once had a doubt
Praise because God woke you up and watched over you at night
Praise because God brought you out of darkness and introduced you to the light
So if you can L.O.L (laugh out loud)
Then you can P.O.L (praise out loud)
And don't worry about what people say, when you praise be **bold** and be proud.

Look Alike

When people say I look like my father, I smile and say thanks for the compliment. And when they say I did a good job with something I first thank my father for my accomplishment. My father gave me a gift, so most definitely I will use it. But growing up I wasn't close to my father so the gift he gave me I would abuse or miss use it. I didn't know the meaning of my gift, never really understand my purpose. So I live a life of selfishness, doing what I thought, some would say my life was worthless. Worthless because of not listening to my father I tried to survive my own way. Using my gifts and talents to try to make a living but, I went about it the wrong way. I used my gift of laughter to talk down on people; I cursed a lot in my speech. Used my writing to lie about things, and that's just to say the least, I learned a hard lesson you play with fire you get burned, but I was stubborn and immature. But note now the lesson was giving and the lesson was learned. My father set me down and showed me different things like; I should use my gifts to build the kingdom not to tear down people or things. Now my life is better, me and my father are getting stronger, and my father is best I wouldn't ask for another

My God

They say the president black. That's cool, but my God is Omni present, and he's been with me BC to AD. That means the past and the present, the alpha and omega, beginning and the end. See I'm a friend of God and he also calls me friend. He always got my back, especially when in need. Even though he allows me to struggle, he takes great care of me. My God is so amazing he even died for me, and then rose again so he could continue his legacy. To go out and preach the gospel and to show he is the king of kings. I think if God had a choice to do it all over, he would do the same thing. I love my God, and I know he loves me and I thank him all the time for always being there for me.

From The Womb

You see everything happens for a reason. I call it destiny: something to which a person is destined. So even before I was born being a poet was the path for me. Growing up I had trouble reading and writing so I wouldn't have guessed being a poet was the thing for me. Until one day after I prayed and I heard God say "I have already planned out your life just put your trust in me". At that moment, I was confused, scared but didn't show it. Kept it all balled up real tight because pride wouldn't let me show it, I prayed for guidance because I didn't know the way and I prayed for knowledge and understanding so when I write I have the right words to say. Never knew something that I was so bad at, will help me to be better at life. But it goes to show the difference between my plans and the plans made from Jesus Christ. Poetry started off as a hobby but then it started to feel like it was my life. I started to live how I was writing and writing how I was living. Everything just felt so right. Till this day I thank God for the gift to write because without it, I couldn't even imagine the things that would be going on in my life.

From The Womb To The Road

Started from the womb now I'm here, and while on this road to success, I have left a lot of people behind and for me to apologize that just wouldn't be fair. To me, you see growing up you lose a lot of family members and peers. One thing I have learned is, to truly walk down the path God has set for me I had to remove things and people to make that road more clear. At times I got discouraged, I was depressed, isolated. Felt abandon, lost, the pain and frustration I was feeling I just couldn't shake it. Break it and though I tried to hide the hurt I just couldn't fake it. Tried to cover of my feelings with different things, but I just couldn't replace it. Gave up on myself a lot because I was going through so much and I just couldn't take it, no more. Tried to forget about things and move on but I had to stand tall and just face it. Learned a lot of faith dealing with what I was going through, had to ask myself over and over did I believe God would help me make it through? Every time my answer would be yes. Always felt I was God's Instrument, and for that I always felt very blessed. So I continued to travel down a road that wasn't so clear, confused by the thought that I was so far away from the end yet I felt the finish line was almost here. Dehydrated, thrusting, for the love of the lord. Equipment with words that kept me fighting and poetry was my sword. The challenges of these road are; never give up or

look back. But I don't have to worry about neither of those things because God paved the way and he's my tour guide, so there's no need to be scared or to turn back.

My Time My Future

You see I knew my time was coming just couldn't pin point the day, man I experienced struggle after struggle plus situations seemed like they were attacking me from every way. Strong holds got stronger, health started getting worst, brush it off like oh well its life I'm just the gift experiencing the curse. Prayed and thank God for my situations because I know somebody else's situations are way worst. I'm not gone lie I'm feeling like a young Job from the bible keeping the faith even though I'm fighting off this hurt. Through struggle comes success thought myself that at a young age, fight no matter how hard things got learned that from my mom and grandma's ways. Working 2 sometimes 3 jobs to provide and take care of their families. Growing up I had everything but learned through hard you can have anything and be whoever you wanted to be. So I took that into consideration thought long and hard, made writing my outlet to talk about the time I've been hurt, bruised and scarred. Came across different obstacles that had me a little confused. Should I jump, crawl, go under or try a different way I had to figure out my next move. Even with the obstacles nothing could hold me, because God told me this is my time and my future so no matter what eventually I will get passed these obstacles so I could tell my story.

Overcoming Obstacles

With overcoming obstacles comes determination and motivation. But in the midst of that, there might be a little stress and frustration. The best thing to do in those times is to pray and trust Jesus, the one we have faith in. In Psalm 138:3 it says, "As soon as I pray, you answer me; you encourage me by giving me strength."(NLT) So in times of loneliness, heartache, and pain, know that our Father can get you through any and everything. So now it's time to smile because God has blessed you this far and has yet to fail. And after God turns your tragedies into your triumphs, you can help someone else by having your own story to tell. Jesus Loves You

Blue Print

It started out as a dream, then I turned it into a brain storm, turned my brain storm to an outline of passion, and then my blue print started to form. I went from a writer and started telling people I was an architect because through my writings, I was building up the kingdom, but I'm now trying to figure out what I'm building next. I'm a home body I like chillin, so I'm a start in my own community. Bring the unsaved to the save; call it a nation day of unity. A lot of time Christians catch themselves preaching to the choir. I say get out your comfort zone, go out to the street and let the unsaved be the fuel to your fire. I'm trying to reach the lost that's what my heart desires, trying to win souls and make disciples and tear down the devils empire. The way I will do that is, I will turn my dreams into a brain storm, turn my brain storm to an outline, and watch my blue print start to form.

From My Pain To My Passion

From my pain to my passion, the change, the relapsing, the questions but never asking, so now I'm living in a lost world. The slow fight to get better, the shrugs of the shoulders, the whatever's; every day my sins are getting greater because I'm still blinded by this cold world. The helping hand I'm not holding had the winning hand, but I'm folding because I can't base my life on a card game. The change in my talk still yet to see it when I walk, so what you see is what's real, so I'm still living the same. Hoping one day to get better but first I have to survive the stormy weather, because at the end of the storm Gods, light will shine greater. My pain will become my passion but in order to get to my passion I had to take on my pain.

Be strong.

Your Dream My Calling

You believe in chasing dreams, I'm just walking in my calling.

You believe in giving up, I was always good in math, so I believe in problem solving.

You believe I got lucky in life, I tell you this is God's vision;

I'm just blessed trying to stay humble and obedient in my everyday living.

You say life is hard, I didn't know it was suppose to be easy.

You value how life should be based off the things you hear and see on TV.

I can't chase my dreams because I never dream about anything good.

I dream about the hurt, the lost, the broken and also the misunderstood.

So instead of chasing my dreams I'm a keep walking patiently in my calling

Because, my dreams are my assignments to the things I need to talk about in my calling.

Well, writing is calling, and I believe I'm pretty good at what I do, and NO!

I don't think I am or want to be the best I just want to do my best at what I do.

My Life My Passion

Let's get this perfectly clear, I'm not a writer I'm a poet, Even though that's not how things seem to appear. If you looked deep into my heart, you'll see this is my life; this is my passion. And if you didn't know, I'm "Gods Instrument" so when I write it comes out in a Godly fashion. You see I didn't have to say "send me I'll go" because I been traveling down this road, to spread the word of the gospel and tell stories that have never been told. So if you think that I do this for money or fame, guess again it's not worth it, because if you take away the fame and money there's still going to be people in the world that is hurting. So for certain my heart bleeds with love and passion for the world. And best believe that I will use the gift that God gave me to help and also bless the world. A wise man once told me, "never put a price on passion because the passion that God has for us cannot be bought, and his love is everlasting." So reevaluate why you do what you do because what I have learned; you never know who's watching and wants to be just like you.

I'm Ready Lord!

My mind racing my thoughts chasing I have move quick.
I'm erasing and replacing the things that kept me in bondage.
The violence, the lust for sex and money, praise God I never did drugs.
The backtracking, the relapsing, Lord I can't do it.
The Godly life, the living right, I'm on my pursuit to it.
Staying focus team Adidas but like Nike I have to just do it.
Stay tuned you will see a different me those things I use to do was just foolish.
Didn't see the light I was on my Stacy Dash, lost, living my life real clueless.
But now I'm ready to move forward I'm willing lord.
Gospel nerdz, 1st Infantry, 100 percent we in this Lord.
We got the armor of God our tongue are our weapon just needs to be a little sharper Lord.
So we deep in your word, so when we speak it comes out in the right order lord.
You gave us these gifts so please just use us Lord.

The time is now it's our time To Take It to Em Lord.

Off To The Races

Off to the races, I smell victory is near, and I'm running faster than usual because they say you run faster when you run out of fear, and I'm scared. But can you hear it? The crowd cheering their clapping me in. All my life people have been calling me a loser, so I'm celebrating after this win. Because they didn't think I could do this, they didn't think I could win, just like they didn't believe Jesus when he said "when I die I will rise in three days so don't be surprise when you see me again." And that's how it happens, crucified, died, and then rose after three. When I heard that story all I can think was two words mission… complete. That story hit something in my body it touched me real deep felt like even though I won the race didn't feel like my mission was complete. So instead of celebrating I went back to the drawing board I had to look deep down inside and ask myself what I was even in the race for. You see God had a mission, he had a plan, and he went forth, but now that I think about it I did it all for self worth. I quickly asked God to forgive me because I went about it the wrong way. And came to the realization that I don't need the lime light, I just need to focus on how God will view me at the end the day. So when you're doing God's work don't worry you might not come in the first place, but if you ask me now I believe that God was

happy with me trying my hardest and just finishing the race.

Lost and Found

It gets hard out here on your lonesome, cause I grew up in a family where family communicated and came to a conclusion that no one wants em. So what am I suppose to do? Didn't have any other options, so I turned to the drugs, and the violence to help me make it through. Now I'm walking down the street with holes in my clothes and two left shoes. Family always told me I wasn't gone be nothing, so why go to school? Pops always said, "don't work too hard for another man" so getting a job was out of the question. Never really knew right from wrong, so there was no second-guessing. You see I always thought that having a child was a blessing, but I experienced child abuse, depression, and now I'm always stressing. See this life got so hard that I couldn't escape, but ever since that first day at that hospital, I knew I was a mistake. You hear about people winning the lottery but why couldn't I get that big break? But I ain't asking for a million dollars, just a hot shower, some clothes and a little bit of food on my plate. Better yet, if I had one wish, I wouldn't wish for no hot shower, no clothes, or even no food on my plate. I would go back in time and look at the day I was born and ask God to erase that date. You see none of this would have happened if I never was born, but God showed me a good lesson that, you got to stay strong when you're walking through that storm.

Controversy

Now I know some of y'all are confused and are questioning your motivation to praise God in this dying world. Questioning God like: How you going to let someone just go in that school and kill all those little boys and girls? Questioning God like: How you going to let somebody go in to the movie theater and in that mall and shoot people just to say they did something? Killing all these innocent people that had nothing to do with nothing. Now I know some of y'all are sad, mad, and I'm angry just like you, but we can't keep blaming Jesus on things that humans do. I guess when there's a tragedy or disaster in the world blaming God is the thing to do huh? But since people say there is no God I guess there isn't any point to even blaming Mohammed or Buddha. I'm just speaking the truth. My advice is if you're a believer just keep on believing. Because God's not the one out there misleading or mistreating. And I'm not trying to be selfish, but for y'all that's blaming when have y'all stopped to thank God that y'all still breathing? There's a lot of killings and other tragedies going on in the world and it's angering me. So let's join our fellow believers in our communities and pray for the things that we don't see on TV. So if you're still confused or questioning your motivation to praise God in this dying world. Ask yourself

This one question, how would your life would be if Christ didn't die for this world?

Stop Lying

Stop lying to the congregation be truthful with them. Sweeping things under the rug that's not doing nothing but hurting them. They walk around the church like nothing is wrong choir director's gay, and the pastor knows it but don't say nothing just up there clapping and singing as the choir director lead that song. Now don't get me wrong I love everyone and I don't have nothing against gays, all I'm saying is God don't like it, and we should try to help the situation instead of keeping things in the closet just so the church won't get looked at a certain way. On another note let's get back to the basic, a lot of churches are built on money and fame let's just face it. Motives all wrong, teaching the half truth, some pastor's do what I called "positive preaching" that's when the say" things are wrong or God don't like it". But don't show it in scripture so where is the proof. I was always told if it's not the whole truth then it's simply not true. So make sure their preaching from the bible and be careful what you are listening to. I'm not out here to try to bash nobody I'm just saying take some time pray and open your eyes. Time to read things for yourself so you too will learn and realize…THE TRUTH!!!!

Broken

This goes out to that broken one that thought he was right but fell in love with the wrong one. Thinking that he was sent from up above she put all her trust in him the boy she so called loved. So they got into a relationship having fun living life. One day they even talked about becoming husband and wife. They laugh together, played together, and even ate together. And at times they didn't have nothing to do they talked and fell asleep on the phone together. You see everything was going good until that one sad day when all the fun stopped, and the love started to fade away. The arguments started, and the tears began to fall, and she left all her friends for him, so she didn't have anyone to call. Now she's all alone with nobody by her side with nothing else to do, she started to pray and ask God why? Why is this happening? What went wrong? Wasn't he sent from you? If so why is our love not strong? Then God spoke and said, "My child I tried to speak to you but you didn't want to listen, and that's why the love you thought you had is now gone and now it's missing." "My child the signs were clear, but you didn't focus in and instead of you putting your trust in me you put all your trust in him." "Now you see why I wanted you to wait and I hope you learned you lesson so next time you won't make the same mistake." Then the girl

spoke and said, "God I want to thank you for showing me who I am and if I ever fall in love again I will put my trust in you and never put my trust in him."

Was It Really Love?

That four letter word have been in my life forever, through the tears and the pain I can depend on that word forever. Every time I hear the word everything just seems so right. It brings smiles and joy to my life everything just feels so right. But when it's gone you feel hurt again, bruised, and scarred like what went wrong? The piano plays and you hear words, but it's a sad lonely song. All alone you thought this four letter word was going to help you make it through but instead it haunted, broke you down and also ruined you. Growing up you thought love was the four letter word you can trust and you can, so trust it because the sad part is the four letter word I talked about in this poem wasn't love it was lust. Don't be confused.

Isn't She Lovely?

*10. Who can find a virtuous and capable wife?
She is more precious than rubies. Proverbs 31:10 NLT*

Ever wonder if you would find that perfect one. A match made in heaven sent from the Holy Spirit, the father and son.

I always wanted to get married ever since a young'n. And I'm started to get more excited because I know that time is coming.

Can't wait to give her my heart hoping it will never get broke into pieces. Instead this love I been holding for years I will soon get to share and release it.

A God fearing woman, a lover, and a best friend, a supporter, a companion, who shares love till the very ends.

Someone who holds you accountable when you're doing wrong, someone that will be there through the good and the bad, who will never leave you alone.

Someone who encourage you to be the best you can and keep fighting with you because she too feels the passion in your heart a feeling that's real deep.

Someone that prays with you, reads with you, someone who genuine loves your life. Someone who knows the true meaning of love like the love we get from Christ.

Someone who knows when you're sad by just looking in your eyes, someone who knows how to be that handkerchief or shoulder because a real man does cry.

Someone who laughs with you and know how to have fun someone you don't have to think twice about because you will know when you have found THE ONE.

A Perfect Gentleman

Husbands love your wives, just as Christ loved the church and gave himself up for her. Ephesians 5:25 NIV

Ever ask yourself if you will find that man, who will love you, care for you, and protect you till the end.

Ever ask yourself if you will find someone that knows how to treat you because he learned by listening to the Holy Spirit the father and the son.

Ever wonder if you will find a man with a plan that will treat you more than a wife but also a loving companion.

Ever wonder if you will find a man that will show you the true definition of love that will not base y'all relationship on material things but will shower you with love from your heart, kisses and hugs.

Ever wonder if you will find a man that will listen to you as you share your feelings that will be there to fill the emptiness and be the piece of your life that was missing.

Ever wonder if you will find a man that would give his whole heart to God so he could give his heart to you.

Well stop wondering and wait that time will come. And when he comes in your life keep him because you might not find another one.

Help Wanted

A young boy was standing on the corner with a sign I could barely read. He had holes in his clothes, no shoes, no socks, so I just assumed the sign said something that he needs. So I pulled up reached out and tried to hand him a five dollar bill. The young boy shook his head no, pushed my hand back. I was shocked, like this can't be real. I drove off puzzled, confused I didn't understand. Why did he do that? Why didn't he take the money from my hand? The next day I saw the young boy but this time I had a twenty dollar bill in my hand. The boy looked at it shook his head no and pushed back my hand once again. I quickly pulled over hopped out my car, and I walked right over. Asked the young boy why are you doing that? What's up with the cold shoulder? The young boy spoke and said, "I have a place to stay," "I have clothes," and "food to eat" "I'm not here for the money, help is what I need." "I'm trying to meet my Lord and savior, but no one will talk to me." "They think because I'm standing on the corner money is what I need." I spoke and said, "I'm sorry I assumed, I should have took the time to ask, but I assumed because when I see people money is all they ask." I hope I can help you now in any way I can, and if I ever see a sign I can't read, I will never assume again. I just got one question for you, "what does your sign really say?"

He said, "It says help wanted I'm trying to meet Jesus can you help in any way?"

Alter Call

Before you read this prayer, I would like you to think about your life. Think about everything you're doing wrong, and everything you're doing right. Have you ever thought about God and what he did for me and you? See Jesus went through the obstacles so that we wouldn't have to jump through any hoops. The only thing you would need to do is ask God into your heart; so he can turn on your light and you won't have to keep living in the dark. Right now this is your opportunity to say this one prayer. After that, you don't have to worry anymore because Jesus will always be there. Now I know you might want to wait until you go to church on Sunday, but tomorrow is never promised and you might not make it another day. I don't want you to just say this if you really don't mean it because God knows your heart, so he's going to know if you really meant it. But now that time has come where you can change your life today and when you read this I ask that you read it loud so God can really hear each word that you say.

The Prayer

God I realize I'm a sinner, and I know you gave your only son to give me a second chance. God I understand that I am not perfect, and I know I will never be perfect. But at this time I want to ask you to forgive me for all of my sins, for the ones I have committed and for the ones that might come about. I would also like to ask you if you can come into my heart so you can show me a new me, and so you can order my steps. God I just want to tell you thank you for everything and AMEN

Bonus Poem

Letter To My Dad

Growing up I wanted a real dad not a father that I was dreaming. But growing up I had an anger problem and every time I would speak about him my mouth would hurt like I was a baby and I was teething. Questioned myself like what's the reason? He would leave me to be another statistic? Another black kid growing up in a home where the father was missing, wishing, one day he would work on being a happy family, but I soon realized there's no such thing as genies so my wishes would never become reality. A sad thing to see, but I soon dried my eyes and had to make myself understand that this is how life has to be. Even though that has affected me for many years, I forgive him and thank him because this has shaped me to be the man I needed to be. And if I have one thing to tell him I learned from all this, its forgiveness. It's the key to life, and I'm thankful for all the times people have forgiven me.

Letter To My Father

Father, I been away, and it's hurting me deeply. You stood by my every day, and I strayed away to the things I thought would complete me. Father we use to be close, long talks with time of laughter, even cried sometimes but that was okay it only lasted for so long and I was much better right after. I never imagined having a father like you giving up everything to take care of your seed, blessed me with different gifts different talents even allowed me to get things of want even if it was something I didn't need. Father I want us to be closer than ever before, and the letter is to say I'm sorry for running away from home, and I'm excited for what we have in stored... Your child God's Instrument

You Can't

You can't hold me back; I refuse to get knocked down.

You can't stop my smile; I refuse to just sit here and frown.

You can't take me back; I refuse to live like I used to.

You can't make me do wrong; I refuse to not do what I am supposed to do.

You can't make me quit; I refuse not to be a winner.

You can't make me sin; I refuse to live life as a sinner.

You can't live my life; only I can, and I will live my life the best way I can…

As a Christian woman

You Can't

You can't hold me back; I refuse to get knocked down.

You can't stop my smile; I refuse to just sit here and frown.

You can't take me back; I refuse to live like I used to.

You can't make me do wrong; I refuse to not do what I am supposed to do.

You can't make me quit; I refuse not to be a winner.

You can't make me sin; I refuse to live life as a sinner.

You can't live my life; only I can, and I will live my life the best way I can…

As a Christian Man

No More

Time to move once again nobody seems to like me. And me staying with one family for more than a year is unlikely. Man this ain't me, having to move from crib to crib because my foster parents blaming something on me that I did not do, but they say I did. Man I wish they could have named me Martin. Then maybe I could have had a dream that everything I'm going through no other kid would have to experience the same thing. But instead I have nightmares, and every day I wake up I'm wondering if there's a foster parent out there that really cares. And guess what's next? My foster parents don't want to work, so they use me as a pay check. For $2000, a month, you can take this kid in your home. And they don't even talk to me so I might as well run away and try to make it on my own. You see, I almost cried when I saw that commercial "there's no place like home" 'cause at the age of two, I never had one 'cause my family left me all alone. All alone in a world that says, "It takes a village to raise a child." But is that really true? I think not, and I feel there's no one out there that knows what to do, but me. So I'm going to do what I have to do until I turn eighteen. Then I'm going to move and start my own group called "I turn nightmares into dreams." And I'm going to make sure no other kids will have to experience the same

things and all their nightmares will be gone. And they will be glad to say that "There's no place like home."

Moments Of My Deepest Regrets

You were the girl that admired me from afar
The one that made me feel like a celebrity and treated me like a star
And somehow we became close, and I got to know you for who you are, And I began calling myself your brother while stringing along your heart
Smile wide as the ocean with a nose the size of Pinocchio's
Saying things like, "Sis you need a winner!" While treating you like my trophy
And as fate would have it, we played the infamous "lets considered us" game
And me knowing your feelings I played the "I have to many issues with trust" game
See my love boat sank once which had me expecting you to float
While my past held on to all of my present wants and my future hopes
And soon you saw I had no intentions to let them go
My heart was bound no matter how much you stretched the rope
I took advantage of you my sister and friend
I couldn't see that on the surface, it took me looking within
I should have never crossed that line in the sand standing

tall without the spine of a man
And years have passed, and they say time tends to heal all wounds
But can minutes really be bandages? Can hours really be Neosporin?
Do days take away the pain of manipulation? Do weeks leave scars?
I guess only time will tell if time can pay the debt of my deepest regrets

I Salute

A ten-TION as I stand with one hand over my heart I raise the other one slowly to my head and I salute for all the soldiers around the world that's fighting and risking their life's while there on that battle field. Things are starting to get real its pitiful to have to see all the kids training to kill or be killed. Every step is critical watch where you're going one wrong step might be your last step but you not knowing. Some days you're crawling on your elbows knees getting dirty, you feel a tear drop and your mind began to worry. Will this be my last day here? Only time can tell Lord please have mercy. You ask the lord to protect you over these struggling years. You're forced to stay up at night because your nightmares have become your reality fears, BOOM! Dang that was a close call with the lord on my side I will fight and stand tall. I reminisce on the time God keep me safe through all my down falls as I thank the lord for my family and friends. I give him a big thanks in advance for protecting me, and I know I will be home to my loved ones again. At ease soldier

Layover

Long wait starting to get a little sleepy can't wait to get home this world is starting to be creepy.
But since I'm waiting might as well get some work done spread the word, share the gospel until my Lord and savior comes.
I use to hate a layover, but this one's a little different. I'm going to make the best of it, try to help the hurt the lost and go to areas where Jesus is missing.
Flights cancelled, everything's expensive, money low, looking at prices mad, taking everything offensive.
Clam down, everything will be just fine. You're on this layover for reason, is what keeps replaying in the back of my mind.
So I hit different terminals, restaurants to see who was waiting just like me. To see if maybe we can hang, chat or maybe have a little bible study. As I searched I started to feel a little out of place. The more I tired the more it felt like a cat and mouse chase. Seems like they were scared to talk to me, seem like everything was fine till I mentioned Jesus that's when people turn their backs to me. I kept trying and trying hoping someone would listen. I went up, I went down, I was on an all around mission. My luck finally came, a woman came up to me and ask what I was doing? She said she had time to listen to me. I said I have a long layover, and I was trying to past, time by helping

people come to Christ and tell them how Christ lives in mines. She said I'm willing to listen and may have a few questions. For weeks, I been thinking about going to church, but I'm tired of second guessing. If Jesus helped you, how I've seen you try to help people, I want in. I'm all alone so it would be nice to have a friend. I said let's sit down, and we can have a talk. The point of this poem was just to say the world is our layover till Jesus return one day so go out your box and share the word even if you get turned down cause you never know whose trying to hear the word in a room filled with thousands. If you just reach one look up and thank God and tell yourself one is better than none. What will you do while on your layover?

Introduction To: Why Me?

The next two pages are poems from my up and coming play titled "Why Me?" I pray that you have a clear mind as you read them. I pray that if you're a person that has experienced what you will read that God has healed you, and you were able to move on with your life. Thanks again for taking the time to read my book. Be looking out for more projects coming soon, your friend God's Instrument

Why Me?

Something happen in my life that I really don't want to share because sometimes in my life I feel alone like no one's there. Who really can I run to? When I'm having different problems, is there anybody out there? Who really can help me solve them? So I searched, and I searched for many months and many years. I felt different feelings. I even experienced different fears. You see my main fear was a man because he used me in many ways. I couldn't even live my life because the thoughts affected me for many days. But still I searched, and I searched to find that one special friend, the one I could tell my story of why I trusted no man. Then one day my searched finally came to an end I found that special person and to my surprise, it was a man. It was a man they call Jesus and he helped me so much. He brought me into His arms, so I felt His love and His grace through His very touch. So I gave my life to God and everything started to come out. But then God asked me that one question, He said, "Who was the man you were talking about?" I said, "That man took my innocence and I don't know why, so every time I see a man a tear forms in my eyes." I really couldn't avoid it I didn't see it coming, but only if I had that one warning, my mind would have told my body to start running. I really couldn't stop him it was really no escape. I tried to scream for help, but it was already too late. You see, I

tried to slip away, but he held me down real tight. And I tried to push him off me, but he was too strong for me to put up a fight. So I'm screaming, and I'm screaming, but in his eyes it was like he didn't even care. And all I could think about is, "I wish someone was there." I really couldn't believe this man was taking my innocence, but I know somebody had to be there, there had to be at least one person that witness this. After it was over, he told me about one other. And I bet he didn't even know that we were birth by the same mother. Still in shock, all I can do was pray and ask God to save me on that very day.

Why Me? Part 2

Something is happening in my life that I really can't explain, like the day I lost my innocence since then my life hasn't been the same. Since that day, I have been lost still yet to be found, and I often question myself why me? Why did my life have to get turned upside down? I never been so hurt, I never felt so much pain. I just wish I can erase the memories the guilt and all shame. Why did he pick me? Why couldn't I fight back? Why was I all alone? Why did I leave the house that day? Why? Why questions began to form. I started to blame myself I tell you the things that happen to me I wouldn't wish that on nobody else. Every time I think about it, it just replays in my head. I cry till I fall asleep but when I wake the visions are still in my head. The hands over my mouth, the ropes that tied my hands and legs, the tears, the black eyes I even picture the blood from between my legs. The consist cry for help that nobody can hear because I'm crying from inside. The thoughts of was this ever going to end or would I even see the outside? It only lasted about five minutes, but five minutes turned to forever. I was released, told myself I wasn't going tell nobody never, ever, ever. Yeah that has happened just hope one day I can release it from my mind and I will be free at last.

To be continued.

Restored

In the beginning, it was stolen. My innocence as a child. And the unwanted grief has strived me to the nights of rubs that made my world seem as a dove. A dive in a pool of blood racing to drink the fountain of dirt. And never ending touches that keep my mouth shut. To protect the private I had known unexamined by other men. Slaved down into a bed of rocks and the legs of jello. All I wanted was for someone to say hello to this girl that hurls every time a man looks at her and not in her eyes. I feel for the girl that has been beat to perfection to please the unpleasable people. Yes, I have found myself in this man. The one that everyone claims to have the master plan. I gave him a chance even though now it's hard to trust because the man that abused me was a man my family loved. For my heart was broken with no seeds to grow, no flowers to water, and no air to breathe. For long I have held this within without shielding truth. No one asked, so I did not tell, but God had other plans. To bring up my testimony to encourage and inspire others. God put peace into me but did not take pieces of my body to do it. And as I shed this truth to you God has bloomed my flowers to prove that He cares and you're not alone in this world of fear. Fear to stand up and yes I too know what you've been through. As I look back now, I can say thank you. Not because I got to experience these things but because I

am saved form them now and these things no longer hold me back from being free. Free through the whips that striped His back. Free through the spit that was spit on His face. Free through the nails that ran through His wrist. I am restored through the sacrifice of Christ amen.

Write Your Own Poem

No_Morellc@yahoo.com

Write Your Own Poem

No_Morellc@yahoo.com

Write Your Own Poem

No_Morellc@yahoo.com

Write Your Own Poem

No_Morellc@yahoo.com

www.ingramcontent.com/pod-product-compliance
Lightning Source LLC
Chambersburg PA
CBHW051927160426
43198CB00012B/2067